KIDS ON EARTH

Wildlife Adventures – Explore The World
Euro Marten Rodent

Sensei Paul David

COPYRIGHT PAGE

Kids On Earth: Wildlife Adventures - Explore The World

Euro Marten Rodent

by Sensei Paul David,

Copyright © 2023

All rights reserved.

978-1-77848-191-8 KoE_WildLife_Amazon_PaperbackBook_euro marten rodent

978-1-77848-190-1 KoE_WildLife_Amazon_eBook_euro marten rodent

978-1-77848-425-4 KoE_Wildlife_Ingram_Paperbackbook_EuroMartenRodent

This book is not authorized for free distribution copying.

www.senseipublishing.com

@senseipublishing
#senseipublishing

Synopsis

This book is an exploration of 30 unique fun facts about the European Marten. This small and curious creature is native to Europe and is one of the most beloved animals in the region. This book covers a variety of topics including the European Marten's habitat, diet, behavior, and anatomy. Additionally, it discusses the European Marten's intelligence, playfulness, and resilience. The book also provides information about the European Marten's vocalizations, metabolism, and ability to climb. It is an excellent resource for children ages 6-12 who are interested in learning about this incredible species.

Get Our FREE Books Now!

kidsonearth.life

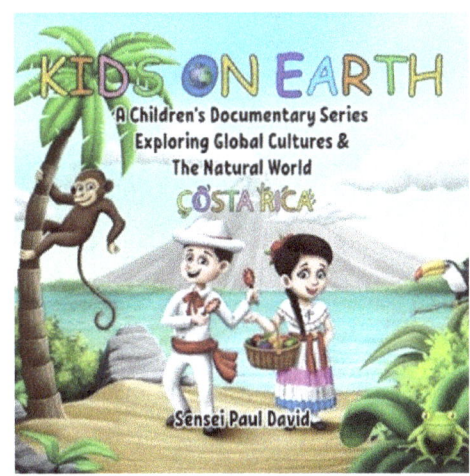

kidsonearth.world

Click Below for Another Book In Each Series

senseipublishing.com/KoE_SERIES   senseipublishing.com/KoE_Wildlife_SERIES

KoE En Español

senseipublishing.com/KoE_SERIES_SPANISH

www.senseipublishing.com

Join Our Publishing Journey!

If you would like to receive FUTURE FREE BOOKS and get to know us better, please click www.senseipublishing.com and join our newsletter by entering your email address in the pop-up box.

Follow Our Blog: senseipauldavid.ca

Follow/Like/Subscribe: Facebook, Instagram, YouTube: @senseipublishing

Scan the QR Code with your phone or tablet to follow us on social media:

Like / Subscribe / Follow

Introduction

Welcome to the wonderful world of the European Marten! This small and curious rodent is native to Europe and is one of the most beloved animals in the region. It is known for its intelligence, playfulness, and beauty. In this book, we will be exploring 30 unique fun facts about this incredible creature. So grab a seat and get ready to learn all about the European Marten!

The European Marten is one of the smallest members of the Mustelidae family, which includes animals like weasels, ferrets, and badgers.

European Martens can be found in a variety of habitats including forests, meadows, and even urban areas.

These animals are omnivorous, meaning they eat both plants and animals.

European Martens have a very loud and distinctive call which can be heard from up to a mile away!

European Martens have a very distinctive smell which is caused by a scent gland near their tail.

They are omnivorous and will eat anything from fruits and nuts to small mammals and birds.

They have a very strong sense of smell which helps them to find food and avoid predators.

Despite their small size, they are incredibly strong and can climb trees and jump from branch to branch.

They are solitary animals and live alone, except when mating.

They are excellent swimmers and can stay underwater for up to 5 minutes at a time.

They have a very high metabolism and need to constantly search for food.

They have a lifespan of up to 10 years in the wild.

European Martens are very intelligent and can learn to recognize human faces.

European Martens have excellent eyesight and can see up to 75 feet away.

European Martens have a very keen sense of smell and can smell food from up to a mile away.

European Martens are excellent climbers and can climb up to 100 feet in a single leap.

They have a unique way of communicating using a combination of body language, scent marking, and vocalizations.

They are incredibly fast and can run up to 30 miles per hour.

They are nocturnal and sleep during the day, coming out at night to search for food.

European Martens have sharp claws which help them climb trees and catch food.

They have thick fur which helps them stay warm in cold temperatures.

They are excellent hunters and can catch their prey in a matter of seconds.

They have thick fur which helps them stay warm in cold temperatures.

They are very territorial and will defend their area from other animals.

European Martens are incredibly playful and can be seen chasing each other and playing tag.

They can jump up to six feet in the air and can swim up to five feet underwater.

They are very social animals and can be seen playing with each other in groups.

European Martens have a wide variety of vocalizations which they use to communicate with each other.

They are very curious animals and will often explore their surroundings when given the opportunity.

They are incredibly resilient and can survive in harsh environments.

Conclusion

We hope you enjoyed learning about the incredible European Marten! This small and curious creature is one of the most beloved animals in Europe. With its intelligence, playfulness, and beauty, it is no wonder why so many people love this creature. We hope that this book has helped to expand your knowledge of the European Marten and that you have a newfound appreciation for this incredible species.

Thank you for reading this book!

If you found this book helpful, I would be grateful if you would **post an honest review on Amazon** so this book can reach other supportive readers like you!

All you need to do is digitally flip to the back and leave your review. Or visit amazon.com/author/senseipauldavid click the correct book cover and click on the blue link next to the yellow stars that say, "customer reviews."

As always…

It's a great day to be alive!

Share Our FREE eBooks Now!

kidsonearth.life

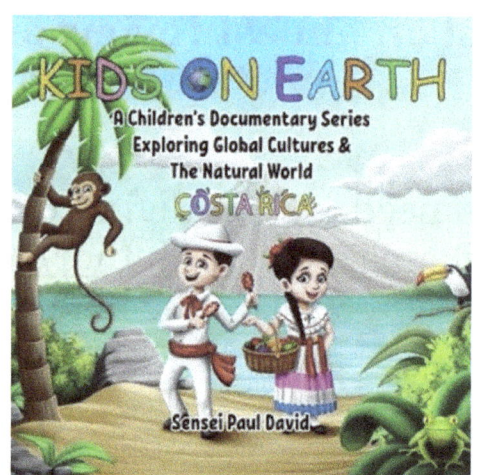

kidsonearth.world

Click Below for Another Book In Each Series

senseipublishing.com/KoE_SERIES

senseipublishing.com/KoE_Wildlife_SERIES

KoE En Español

senseipublishing.com/KoE_SERIES_SPANISH

www.senseipublishing.com

www.senseipublishing.com

@senseipublishing
#senseipublishing

Check out our **recommendations** for other books for adults & kids plus other great resources by visiting
www.senseipublishing.com/resources/

Join Our Publishing Journey!

If you would like to receive FREE BOOKS and special offers, please visit www.senseipublishing.com and join our newsletter by entering your email address in the pop-up box

Follow Our Engaging Blog NOW!
senseipauldavid.ca

Get Our FREE Books Today!

Click & Share the Links Below

FREE Kids Books

lifeofbailey.senseipublishing.com

kidsonearth.senseipublishing.com

FREE Self-Development Book

senseiselfdevelopment.senseipublishing.com

FREE BONUS!!!
Experience Over 25 FREE Engaging Guided Meditations!

Prized Skills & Practices for Adults & Kids. Help Restore Deep Sleep, Lower Stress, Improve Posture, Navigate Uncertainty & More.

Download the Free Insight Timer App and click the link below:
http://insig.ht/sensei_paul

About Sensei Publishing

Sensei Publishing commits itself to helping people of all ages transform into better versions of themselves by providing high-quality and research-based self-development books with an emphasis on mental health and guided meditations. Sensei Publishing offers well-written e-books, audiobooks, paperbacks, and online courses that simplify complicated but practical topics in line with its mission to inspire people toward positive transformation.

It's a great day to be alive!

About the Author

I create simple & transformative eBooks & Guided Meditations for Adults & Children proven to help navigate uncertainty, solve niche problems & bring families closer together.

I'm a former finance project manager, private pilot, jiu-jitsu instructor, musician & former University of Toronto Fitness Trainer. I prefer a science-based approach to focus on these & other areas in my life to stay humble & hungry to evolve. I hope you enjoy my work and I'd love to hear your feedback.

- It's a great day to be alive!
Sensei Paul David

Scan & Follow/Like/Subscribe: Facebook, Instagram, YouTube: @senseipublishing

Scan using your phone/iPad camera for Social Media
Visit us at www.senseipublishing.com and sign up for our newsletter to learn more about our exciting books and to experience our FREE Guided Meditations for Kids & Adults.

www.ingramcontent.com/pod-product-compliance
Lightning Source LLC
Chambersburg PA
CBHW080616110526
44587CB00040BB/3727